ONE STOP SHORT OF
BARKING

ONE STOP SHORT OF
BARKING

Uncovering the London Underground

Mecca Ibrahim

NEW HOLLAND

Contents

① Ready to depart

Every day almost three million people pack themselves into little metal carriages to be transported around London. Though the operators have had more than a hundred years to refine the design, these little metal carriages remain hot, overcrowded, under-funded and dirty and their owners are still unable to recognise the word 'timetable'.

Hate it or hate it, the London Underground is a routine part of many Londoners' existence, a daily torture they can't imagine being without. The relationship between commuter and Tube is one so unhappy that it would daunt even the bravest of marriage counsellors.

But knowledge is power and this book will arm you with everything you need to navigate the world's oldest subterranean transport system with success – and teach you a few things you'll probably wish you hadn't learned.

Throughout the book you'll find anecdotes and stories unearthed by the *One Stop Short of Barking* spies, who have roamed the Underground tirelessly in search of fantastic tales and amazing quotes about everyday journeys.

This is a passenger announcement

You'll also find genuine nuggets of wisdom as broadcast over the network's public address system by London Underground staff to help you on your way. Just as you hear them on the Tube, these are of no practical use at all, but if nothing else they give the impression that there's a human being working out there somewhere on the system.

At least it's easier to hear the drivers and guards now than it was a hundred years ago. Picture the scene in 1907: carriages were nicknamed 'padded cells' with their ventilation slit windows situated high above the heavily-upholstered seats. Without a view, passengers relied on the guards to call out the stops. The noise made it hard to hear and anyone from out of town had a problem understanding the London accent. 'Hurl's Court!' (Earl's Court), 'Ampstead!' (Hampstead), 'Marblarch!' (Marble Arch). Real windows were installed so that passengers could see where to get off instead.

Are we there yet?

This led to the guards having little to announce. Today, the drivers do the talking, but there's rarely much of it. A pre-recorded, Big Brother-style voice booms 'Mind the gap' and 'Stand clear of the doors'. Then there's the computer-controlled, crystal-clear Sonia (Sonia: she gets *on yer* nerves) to announce the station name. So what's a driver to say?

Over the years a collection of driver and station assistant announcements have been reported to the website www.goingunder ground.net. The people driving us to and from work are only human and, like us, they have frustrations with the system. Some sound near suicidal and some shrug off the delays with that cruel humour, sarcasm and irony which is unique to Londoners. As you rattle through this book from stop to stop, you'll spot the

Welcome aboard the Flintstones railway, once I get my feet on the floor and start running we should be on our way.

'A horse walks into a Tube...'

occasional quote from that other underground system with its alternative map: the Irony Line, the Frustration Line, the Isn't-Life-Hell Line and the ever-popular Comedian Line.

Time to get on board with the commuter's version of *Alice in Wonderland*, pass right down the carriage to meet a whole host of glad, sad and mad characters and change at the next stop for hints, tips, trials and tribulations and the secrets of unspoken passenger rules.

With a bit of luck, you won't be *One Stop Short of Barking* by the end.

This is Knightsbridge Station. All change here for Mr Fayed's little corner shop.

A potted history of the Tube

1843 Charles Pearson thinks: 'I'll invent the Tube.' As he's solicitor to the City of London, people listen to him.

1844 Pearson's underground railway plans are satirised in *Punch* magazine: 'It is believed that much expense may be saved by taking advantage of areas, kitchens and coal holes already made, through which the trains may run without much inconvenience to the owners, by making a judicious arrangement of the timetable.' From this it's clear that the Tube might be underway but satire has a long way to go.

1852 Pearson explains that what he's after is 'a frequent, rapid, functional and cheap inter-communication between City and the suburbs without courting dangerous collisions by communing on the same lines, creeping goods wagons with flying expresses and mixing up erratic excursionists with the migratory population of the City.' Like all solicitors, he is paid by the word.

1860 First tube shafts are sunk.

1863 Metropolitan and District Railway, the world's first underground railway, opens – fast workers, the Victorians.

1879 A pharmacist on Gower Street, near the British Museum, sells up to 20 bottles a day of Metropolitan Mixture to help people suffering from the effects of travelling on the Tube.

1884 The Circle Line opens. *The Times* reports, 'A journey from Kings Cross to Baker Street is a form of mild torture which no person would undergo if he could conveniently help it.'

1887 *Daily Express* editor RD Blumenfeld writes, 'I had my first experience of Hades today… I got into the Underground railway at Baker Street.' Undeterred, his son, the future Sir John Eliot, will go on to become chairman of London Transport in the 1950s.

1890 City and South London Railway, the world's first electric underground railway,

'Room for one more?'

opens. It is christened the 'Sardine Box Railway' by *Punch*. 'It was so packed with people that getting in or out was a regular scrimmage. We entirely endorse the railway company's advertisement in that it is the "warmest line in London".'

1901 A new chairman of the Central London Railway is appointed. The womanising, embezzling, bribing American, Charles Tyson 'buy up old junk, fix it up a little and unload it upon other fellows' Yerkes is a real JR Ewing of the Tube.

1908 The slogan 'Underground to Anywhere, Quickest Way, Cheapest Fare' appears on tube maps. The princely sum of £10 is awarded to its author, Edwin Parrington, aged 14.

1926 First suicide pits appear – where the rails are raised, extra space is provided underneath the tracks. The change follows a Westminster coroner's comment that there is 'something about the roar and rush of a Tube train which [was] terribly fascinating to a person if he were alone on the platform.'

1933 The British Museum station is closed. *The Times* offers a reward to anyone prepared to sleep overnight at the station which is said to be haunted by the spectre of an Egyptian mummy. No one takes up the offer.

NO NEED TO ASK A P'LICEMAN!

'Can't you read the map, Madam!'

1936 WJ Kelley, Labour MP for Rochdale, on a Bill to extend the Edgware Line: 'Young girls and men are crowded in such a way that the question of decency even comes up.'

1941 Billy Brown – 'the world's most exemplary passenger' – is created by London Transport to give wartime instructions to commuters in verse. He moves the *Daily Mail* to respond:

'But you chronic putter-righter
Interfering little blighter
Some day very soon, by heck
Billy Brown – I'll wring your neck.'

1955 Chairman of London Transport, Sir John Eliot, helpfully responds to reports of passenger discomfort. 'They are not crammed in. They cram themselves in.'

To the gentleman wearing the long grey coat trying to get on the second carriage, what part of 'stand clear of the doors' don't you understand?

1960 Future TV presenter and best-selling author Clive James takes a psychological test as part of the process of becoming a London Underground guard. He fails.

1987 The Queen's official opening of the Docklands Light Railway with its driverless trains is briefly delayed as the computer doesn't let it leave two minutes early.

1996 The £900 million Jubilee Line Extension linking London to the Millennium Dome is due to be finished. It isn't.

1999 It's time to see whether predictions made by Professor Archibald Montgomery Low in 1914 have come to pass. Writing in *Trains, Omnibuses and Trams*, he foresaw 100 mph trains, mobile phones, solar energy, Eurostar and the Travelcard... and an end to spitting on the Tube. 'In 1999, every station will have comfortable waiting rooms, with all the trains, the news of the moment – and perhaps the picture of the moment – thrown upon artistically illuminated screens.'

1999 The Jubilee Line Extension finally opens at a cost of more than £3.5 billion. John Self, general manager, says, 'True, it has taken longer and cost more than first thought... We have suffered with the rest of London, knowing that we had the best piece of rail estate housed in buildings as big and beautiful as cathedrals. We made the jokes ourselves: "It's no good having the finest churches in the world, if no one can come in to pray".'

Right: *'So where are the comfortable waiting rooms?'*

This train is all stations to Upminster with the exception of Cannon Street, which does not stop there on Saturdays due to total lack of interest.

Tube etiquette includes both official Underground rules and the unspoken passenger lore which exists to make Tube travel harmonious and comfortable or, when all else fails, almost bearable. These are the rules that ensure millions of passengers travel round 275 stations on 3,988 tube carriages every single day without killing each other.

How should you travel to ensure the least inconvenience caused to your fellow passengers? How do you avoid invading their personal space or looking at them in the wrong way? London Underground rules and Tube etiquette have naturally evolved in all capital-dwellers over more than a hundred years of Tube travel. Woe betide any out-of-towner who doesn't follow the code – even if they don't know what it is.

> **Welcome to the Waterloo and City Line. Sights to observe on the journey are, to your right, black walls and to your left, black walls. We will shortly be arriving at Waterloo where this train will terminate. We would like to offer you a glass of champagne on arrival and the platform will be lined with lapdancers for your entertainment – have a good weekend.**

RULE 1: don't read over your fellow traveller's shoulders

Tube train seats are cramped and close together. When they're full, you'll have to strap-hang. But wherever you're squashed and however fascinating other commuters' books or newspapers might be, people can always tell if you are reading over their shoulder. They will think you are a cheapskate who can't be bothered to buy your own reading material. They will also worry about the judgement you'll be making about them when assessing their reading material.

If you really must read over someone's shoulders, pick a decent line, where you are likely to see something juicy. Lines frequented by lawyers are excellent. Go for the District Line, as it goes into Temple, and the Central Line as it goes into Chancery Lane. You'll be rubbing shoulders with lots of lawyers and barristers carrying their 'briefs' or 'cases' – or whatever they call them.

> **Please stand clear of the doors. This is a customer announcement, please note that the big slidy things are the doors, the big slidy things are the doors.**

Maybe one day you'll be on the jury of the case you happen to be glancing at that morning. Or perhaps the person whose material you're reading will turn out to be a key witness and then you'll be able to sue the hell out of the lawyer for displaying confidential items.

Remember, Metro, *the commuter's newspaper, is free.*

RULE 2: don't fall asleep on your neighbour

One of the worst things about falling asleep on the Tube is that most of the time you look like a complete idiot. You can see it in other people who drop off – they're drooling, snoring and – worst of all – some insist on leaning on the person next to them. Some of these human pillows are very polite and just try to wriggle over a bit and hope that the sleeper will wake. Be warned: this does not stop the serious sleeper. You need to elbow them sharply in the side and then look straight ahead. Once awoken, they will hopefully realise what they were doing and try to stay awake or at least not use you as a comfy cushion.

An elegant lady of a certain age once fell asleep on the District Line and woke only when the train arrived at the end of the line – Upminster. The lady enquired in her poshest tones, 'Is this Aldgate East?' The guard immediately replied, 'Nah, lady, it's all git aht.'

I do apologise for the delay to your service. I know you're all dying to get home, unless, of course, you happen to be married to my ex-wife, in which case you'll want to cross over to the westbound platform and go in the opposite direction.

Please note that the beeping noise coming from the doors means that the doors are about to close. It does not mean throw yourself or your bags into the doors.

Right: *An extreme case of Tube slumber.*

RULE 3: stand clear of the closing doors

This is an official rule and made with very good reason. Many believe the Tube train doors were invented by a direct descendent of Joseph Guillotin. A whole range of appendages are regularly trapped in the closing doors, including bags, coats, arms, legs, children, briefcases, bottoms and heads. You may have to wait an eternity for the next train to come along (particularly if you're travelling on the Northern Line), but sometimes it isn't worth the hassle of hurling yourself onto the train at the mercy of the closing jaws.

Strangely, the minute you want the doors to close shut for good, they will miraculously spring open again, in time to let on some undesirable. This is often an obese, perspiring man with halitosis, lumbering on with his flatulent growling dog, who'll then spend the rest of the journey pressed up intimately against you.

'We don't want to separate friends, but...'

'Keep your appendages inside the doors, please!'

RULE 4: don't get caught short on the tube

It appears that when a man's got to go, he's got to go. Toilets on Tube stations are as common as smiling station assistants, so you may have to improvise. When one train was waiting to leave Aldgate station, a man picked up a beer bottle and strolled over to the open doors. To giggles from the rest of the passengers, the man proceeded to urinate into the bottle with his 'equipment' poking out of the doors (definitely a case of someone who needed to listen to the announcement 'stand clear of the closing doors'). When he finished, he zipped up his flies and put the full bottle on the edge of the platform.

RULE 5: your bag is not entitled to a seat

You don't buy a ticket for your bag (you'd have been the victim of a rip-off if you did), so don't think you are entitled to place your bag on the seat next to you. You will be subject to angry looks and abuse when other passengers want to take the seat. The Queen is an obvious exception to this rule. But in her case it's likely that one of her aides did actually pay for this VIP's VIB (Very Important Bag).

> **When the gentleman urinating on platform three has finished, would he ask the attendant for a mop and bucket. Thank you.**

RULE 6: men, shut your legs

Despite evidence to the contrary, it is possible for men to sit on the Tube without spreading their legs so widely that it seems they suffer from womb envy and are trying to experience the joys of child birth. Perhaps inconvenienced ladies should not moan about the lack of space, but instead assist these gents by patting their hands and yelling, 'Push!'

In Japan, an official rule prohibits the splaying of legs akimbo and stickers warning of this are placed throughout the subway system. But perhaps men can't help it. Maybe the real reason that they sit with their legs apart is that their limbs are affected by special magnetic fibres on the upholstery of the seats. It could be that these interact with testosterone to provide an anti-magnetic outward force.

RULE 7: escalator etiquette

This is the official rule which tourists most often break, driving commuters mad. When office workers are in a rush and are trying to hurl themselves down the escalator like kamikaze-bungee-jumping-bobsleighers, someone standing on the left-hand side of the escalator is a positive danger. There are signs on every escalator reminding people to stand on the right and it's best to think of it as equivalent to driving on the wrong side of the road. This is not merely etiquette – it's a matter of survival.

At least it's clearer than the rule that 'dogs must be carried' on the escalator. Having read this odd instruction, tourists can often be seen standing in confused huddles before looking around for a mobile pet shop from where they can choose a suitable furry friend to take on board the escalator.

PLEASE STAND ON THE RIGHT
OF THE ESCALATOR

RULE 8: don't look at anyone

Even though you are in very, very, very close proximity to your fellow travellers, you must try not to look at anyone on the Tube and you must do anything to avoid eye contact. Fiddle with your watch. File your nails. Read the ads (why else are they there?). If we were supposed to look at our fellow travellers, the *Metro* morning commuting newspaper wouldn't be given away at every station and the capital's own journal, the *Evening Standard*, wouldn't be there for us to buy on the way home, as there is little other use for them.

The main reason to avoid eye contact is to escape the attention of potential nutters. They will insist on talking to you and you will become the reluctant star of the carriage because talking on the tube is strictly forbidden.

> To the guy who has decided to defecate at the end of platform two – please be aware that all the rest of the passengers waiting for their trains know you are there and you will have to walk past them to leave the station. There is no other means of escape.

Above: *Getting to know you...*

Right: *A newspaper is the ideal wall to hide behind.*

RULE 9: when you can speak on the Tube

The only acceptable time to communicate without being saddled with the nutter label is when you want to find out if someone has finished with their copy of *Metro*. This free morning newspaper is basically the previous night's *Evening Standard* in a digestible format without the acerbic television column written by Victor Lewis-Smith. The advent of *Metro* has opened a whole floodgate of acceptable conversations.

Many people take a discarded *Metro* without speaking, which is fine if it's on the seat next to you. Others grab discarded copies from the little ledge behind the seats. A simple 'excuse me' before fumbling around behind someone's back is appropriate in situations like this. If someone has literally just finished reading, it is good etiquette to say: 'Isitalrightifitakeyourmetro?' The phrase, when perfected, only takes two seconds to mutter.

Mind the doors. Yes, you, the woman in the long, brown coat, love. I suggest you should shave your legs in future, it'll stop the hairs getting caught in the doors. Look at her everyone! Mingin'!

Covent Garden has been closed due to overcrowding. Please alight at Leicester Square and wander around aimlessly with your huge rucksacks until you get to your destination.

RULE 10: have your tickets ready at the exit

There is nothing more annoying than to be close to escaping the confines of the Tube to the fresh air above and then getting stuck behind someone who spends half an hour trying to find their ticket. This is particularly galling when you hastily put your own ticket in the swipe gates and the bewildered passenger in front wonders why the barrier gates have magically opened. They will blithely step through, leaving you stranded on the other side when the barriers slam shut again. You then have to face the prospect of a long-winded argument with a station assistant, as tickets are not designed to go through twice.

'I have got it.'

'Don't rush me.'

'It's in here somewhere.'

'Aha! Always in the last place I look.'

All the best characters in the Tube's history have stories surrounded in mystery and obscured by the gossip of generations of Londoners who have no time for anything as dull as the unadorned truth behind an atmospheric tale. But take any of these slices of Underground life and, once you dig deeper, you'll learn that the real facts in these cases are often even more strange.

For something as integral and old a part of London as the Tube, it's only natural that there have been as many eccentric staff as passengers, that all life (including birth) goes on down there and that the network plays a key part in the art and literature created about the capital. Its champions, innovators and most distinctive users could take up a book in themselves. Here's an introduction to some of the finest.

Sorry, ladies and gentlemen, we'll have to wait here for a bit. I've been told a computer has fallen off a table somewhere and all the signals have gone wrong.

The Orson Welles of the Underground

In America, the classic Orson Welles radio recording of *The War of the Worlds* was produced with such conviction that millions fled screaming to the hills, believing they were about to be invaded by aliens. It's not so well known, but the Tube has its own version that more than matches Orson's for drama.

In 1897, Londoners were terrorised by *To-Day* magazine's weekly serialisation of the tale of a murderer who used the carriages of the Tube as his stamping ground. Each Tuesday without fail, the murderer would strike a lone passenger slumped in a corner seat. The author, a mysterious freelance correspondent called John Oxenham, would dispatch each instalment from an address in Scotland. He used short clipped sentences and pretend newspaper reports to paint a picture so believable that passenger numbers dropped dramatically on Tuesday nights. Oxenham gleefully played on the public's reaction in the story, warning that 'travel on the Underground is less attractive than of yore and the homely bus is rising in public estimation... a cold-blooded murderer is at large in our midst, and travellers on that all-times depressing Line (the District) are completely at his mercy'.

To-Day relished the unease and gossip resulting from its gruesome tale and reprinted a cartoon, reportedly from *Punch*, in which a city gent was seen to boast that he had travelled in a District Line carriage alone. Around our hero ladies were depicted swooning at his story 'while the season's lions scowl at him from a distance and twirl their moustaches and growl in their neglected corners'.

London Underground big wigs were tearing their hair out at all the fuss by the fourth instalment and wrote a formal letter of complaint to the magazine's editor, humorist and general wag, Jerome K Jerome. Caught between a rise in the publication's sales and the weight of the London Underground management, Jerome sought the advice of his

Right: Buses filled as fast as Tube seats emptied

quietly-spoken business manager. This was former grocer William Dunkerley, who said that he had heard the series was coming to an end and the location would switch from London's grime to a cruise boat heading for Australia. Jerome shrugged his shoulders and decided to let the serialisation run its course. Over time, just as Dunkerley predicted, the setting dramatically changed.

When it came to the finale, it did indeed take place on the high seas, with the murderer coming to a satisfyingly grisly end. Passenger numbers on the 'all-times depressing' District Line crept back to normal. Two years later, it was revealed that John Oxenham was actually a nom de plume of mild-mannered business manager, William Dunkerley.

> **Please leave your valuables on the train and I will collect them at the end of my shift.**

The escalator tester

Now they are so much part of the Tube system, we don't give escalators a second thought, at least, not until they break down. But back in 1911, when escalators first made their shuddery debut at Earl's Court station, the public were sceptical. Who could blame them? A great wooden contraption with ugly teeth on which genteel Edwardian ladies were supposed to place their dainty feet with great care to be transported from platform to exit. Would their feet be trapped? Would gentlemen's spats be splattered?

Enter 'Bumper' Harris, a man employed by the Underground's management to demonstrate how easy it was to travel on the escalators. Not only were these early escalators made of wood, but so was one of Bumper's legs, which led to much speculation from a not entirely reassured public as to how Bumper had lost the limb. Undeterred, Bumper showed how easy it was to glide up and down each day.

Right: *Bumper arrives for work*

By 1913, he had won the public over and escalators became a tourist attraction in their own right. People deliberately stopped at Earl's Court just to try out the stairs. A second escalator was put into Paddington station and passengers were directed to it by staff using megaphones, bellowing 'This way to everywhere! Moving staircase in operation – the world's wonder!'

There is now some speculation as to whether the Underground actually employed Bumper to do his great job. One of his relatives reported to the London Transport Museum

> **I apologise for the delay leaving the station, ladies and gentlemen, this is due to a passenger masturbating on the train at Edgware Road. Someone has activated the alarm and he is being removed from the train.**

Bumper sleeping on the job.

that he was never paid. Think about it though. What sort of a man would happily travel up and down escalators just for the hell of it? As it turned out, the sort of man who then went on to retire to Gloucestershire, far away from the rackety stairs, where he started a successful business making violins and cider.

> There are now only six shopping days left before Christmas and everyone is getting in the mood for festivities. If any of you would like to send me a card, my name is Richard. I usually do this run on the Jubilee Line and you can find me at the front of the train.

The Tube's first-born

Hardly anyone has given birth on a Tube train, which is handy as you cannot imagine drivers making great midwives. But it does happen. In 1924, it was towels, hot water and cigars all round when a baby girl was born in the carriage of a Bakerloo train. The press had a field day, reporting that she was christened Thelma Ursula Beatrice Eleanor (TUBE). In fact, she was really given the name Marie Cordery, as she revealed on a TV programme at the ripe old age of 76, when she also reported that she didn't like travelling on the Underground. Old spoilsport.

She would have been much more likely to have an exotic name if the birth took place today. Picture the priest: 'I baptise you Temple Upney Beckton-Euston.' Why stop there? Following the example of David and Victoria Beckham naming their child after the site of conception, New York's Brooklyn, think of the names kids could have as reminders of their origins in empty (hopefully) carriages. You can almost hear the cries of young mothers: 'Balham, your tea's getting cold' or 'Osterley and Plaistow – tidy your rooms now'.

Getting it mapped out

The Tube map is one of the most recognisable symbols of London. Not only are millions of maps printed, but the design is licensed and reproduced over 60 million times each year to adorn T-shirts, ironing boards, umbrellas, boxer shorts, shower curtains and much more. Bearing little geographical relation to real distances between stations, the map nevertheless helps us navigate the gigantic system. It has also confused more than a few tourists on the way. As travel writer Bill Bryson pointed out, a non-Londoner using the map to get from, say, Bank to Mansion House station would understandably board a Central Line train to Liverpool Street, merrily transfer to the Circle Line and continue for another five stops, getting off the train at Mansion House – exactly 200 yards down the street from where they first started.

Harry Beck in happier days.

Let's meet the man responsible for the map we know and love. In 1931, Harry Beck, a 29-year-old draughtsman, was wondering why the sprawling, geographically-correct map of the time was so hard to follow. He realised that it didn't need to be so literal, straightened some of the lines and made the distances between

Ladies and gentlemen, we will shortly be arriving at Waterloo, then I think we will carry right on through the Channel tunnel and spend the weekend in Paris.

stations more regular. This was the simple, neat and tidy map that is largely unchanged today. But so simple and tidy was it that when first presented to London Transport it was rejected for being 'too revolutionary'.

Beck persisted and, influenced by the recession, the powers that be decided to give the map a go in 1933. It was a phenomenal success and Beck was paid five guineas for his design (about £200 today) which, unfortunately for Harry, included the copyright. He later secured a full time job with London Transport, where he happily tweaked, amended and refined the map for the next 20 years.

When he eventually left London Transport, Beck did so under the understanding that any changes to the map's design would be made by him. Enter Harold Hutchinson in 1960, a mere publicity officer who produced what Beck thought was a travesty of the map – a spiky, ugly effort which proved widely unpopular and was quickly dropped. But the seeds of discontent were sown. Beck entered into a long, bitter correspondence with London Transport and became obsessed with the design for the rest of his life. His wife used to find little drawings of the map tucked under his pillow when she made the bed and his niece remembers visiting him while he was crawling over giant floor-sized versions, continually making alterations to his beloved diagram. In the late 1990s, his services were given belated official recognition with a plaque at Finchley Central station, near to where Beck lived, and a replica of his original map.

The map inspired a Turner Prize-shortlisted work called 'The Great Bear' by artist Simon Patterson. This work takes the map and replaces the names of stations with those of artists, philosophers, comedians and celebrities. It fetched almost £15,000 at auction. Fifteen grand for a spoof! That must have been down to what Patterson's Lisson Gallery biography refers to as 'the playful subversion of familiar classification systems [drawing] unexpected and extraordinary connections between people, facts and ideas by fusing recognisable visual forms with incongruous conceptual associations'. Harry would have been proud.

I am the captain of your train and we will be departing shortly. We will be cruising at an altitude of approximately zero feet and our scheduled arrival time in Morden is 3.15 pm. The temperature in Morden is approximately 15 degrees Celsius and Morden is in the same time zone as Mill Hill East, so there's no need to adjust your watches.

Left: *Service as normal.*

Right: *Trying to make sense of the map.*

Contrary to popular opinion, we are not the only living creatures that use the London Underground. From pigeons, rats and stray dogs to the occasional water buffalo, using the Tube can, at times, seem more like taking a stroll round London Zoo than climbing aboard the cramped, claustrophobic train ride to hell that we've come to know and love.

There are a plethora of our feathered (or furry or scaly) friends frequenting the Underground at any one time. Here are some examples, all of them with different reasons for being on the Tube – some arrive there by accident, many have a purpose. But none of them have a valid travelcard.

> **Go on then, stuff yourselves in like sardines, see if I care, I'm going home.**

Cows are not common commuters.

Passenger pigeons

Who's that beady-eyed passenger standing next to you, wearing a dirty grey suit and waiting patiently for the doors to slide open? *Columba Livia*, that's who – better known as the common pigeon. For many years now, countless London pigeons (a breed similar to the common pigeon, but less friendly and always in more of a hurry) have been spotted flying onto trains – typically near the end of lines in suburban areas – and hanging around on the carriages, ignoring passengers, calmly pecking at food on the floor and then departing one or two stops down the line. And while the orthodox view is that in scrounging for food they accidentally find themselves on unplanned trips, there are plenty who believe that these pigeons have actually planned their itineraries.

When reporting on this phenomenon in 1995, *New Scientist* went as far as to suggest that there were too many sightings of these pigeon journeys for them to be purely accidental and that the birds were 'travelling with intent'. This was not 'necessarily motivated by hunger or ignorance'. Or as one commuter reported: 'I saw one once get on at Gunnersbury. When the train pulled in at Stamford Brook, the pigeon waddled over to the door and looked expectantly at it. Since there was no one on the other side, a woman got up and opened the door for the bird, which flew off... I got the distinct impression that the pigeon had done that journey before.'

Other city-dwelling birds are less bold. The once ubiquitous sparrows have been noted at the end of some lines, but they never seem cheeky enough to venture into the cars, instead hopping around on the platform while looking longingly inside. And, despite recent reports of a flock of lapwings occupying the Central Line from Holborn to Notting Hill, it seems that in the world of feathered commuters, the pigeon is still top, er, dog.

Opposite and below: *The quickest way to travel...*

To the person skateboarding down the southbound platform of the Northern Line – I suggest that you stop. There are approximately 640 volts going through the line beneath you, as you will discover if you fall off the skateboard.

Roaming rodents

Ever seen a little shape scuttling at great speed under the tracks or dashing between seats down the side of a platform? Contrary to folk legend, this is not a rat, just the common brown (and the dirt and dust makes it very, very dark indeed) mouse, or *Mus Musculus*.

A good reason to mind the gap.

If you'd like to see them darting around like clockwork toys, the best places for mouse spotting are to be found wherever food wrappers are likely to be dropped. Find a station that has lots of fast food chains and you'll be in luck. Waterloo is particularly good. When you've just got off the Eurostar and are heading northbound on the Bakerloo line, the British mouse will give you that 'Welcome back to lovely, grimy old England' homecoming.

You can become quite fascinated and hypnotised by the little blighters zooming around, but mouse-watching is frowned on by Tube staff. Once, a couple of kids engaged in peering at rodents were surprised to hear a voice booming over the tannoy at them:

'This is an announcement for the two children near the edge of the platform. Please do not stare at the mice under the tracks, as they are in fact Albanian killer mice and very dangerous. Please stand well back from the platform edge.'

As the kids stopped looking and sheepishly backed away, the same voice came back over the system: 'This is an announcement for the mice on the station: "Eek, eek, eek, eek, eek, eek!" Thank you.'

Londoners have not always been so kind to the Tube's resident rodents. Rat catchers complete with ferrets were employed right up until the 1940s. Bringing us up to date, rats appear in a 1998 computer game with a level set on the Underground. In *Tomb Raider 3: the Adventures of Lara Croft*, our heroine has to shoot several rabid-looking specimens on her travels.

> **Please allow the doors to close. Try not to confuse this with 'please hold the doors open'. The two are distinct and separate instructions.**

THE RatSwine

WOOHOOO!

TRAIN SURFING IS FUN...

... JUST WATCH OUT FOR THOSE TUNNELS !!!

Even if rats have been driven out of the Tube, it's still estimated that there are ten million living under London. Ultrasonic sound is used by pest controllers to drive them mad so that they knock themselves out on sewer walls in a head-banging frenzy. Perhaps the tinny noises from Walkmans on the Tube may turn out to be handy after all.

> **The hilarious gentleman who just showed me his bum, can I suggest that you join a gym or go on a diet before waving it around in future.**

A successful day's rat-catching on the rails of London Undergrou

Metropolitan mosquitoes

A whole new species of creature is evolving on the London Underground (in addition to the breed of musician known as the common busker). The Underground mossie has so many physical differences from the common overground variety that the two are reluctant to mate.

When mosquitoes originally ventured underground, they were fans of bird blood. Not finding as many pigeons on the Tube as they'd like, they decided to branch out into rodent and human fare. Commuters sheltering on the Tube in the Second World War were a particular delicacy.

Mosquito-mad scientists have also found genetic differences between mossies on different Tube lines. Conditions on the network are perfect for rapid breeding of mosquitoes. It's hot, sweaty and there are often pools of stagnant water which provide the perfect courting ground for the little midges. At least one group of passengers is satisfied with the conditions on the Tube.

A possible home for mossies.

5 Play 'Streets of London' for me

Let us now enter a strange subterranean auditioning ground. Busking musicians can be heard each day at the bottom of escalators and in Tube corridors. Some still illegally perform in the carriages themselves. So, will you hear the next Madonna or just some mad old prima donna?

Beggars are operating on this train. Please do not encourage these professional beggars. If you have any spare change, please give it to a registered charity. Failing that, give it to me.

No smiling, no talking...

London's most famous underground buskers have been forced overground by laws which have legalised busking, but only for musicians who pass an audition and play at designated areas on 12 stations on the Tube. And they're certainly not allowed in the carriages.

It's meant the loss of some familiar faces. For more than 20 years, passengers on the Richmond end of the District Line were 'entertained' by the 'If you can't have a shave in the toilet, where can you have a shave?' duo.

Two men – who were simply old enough to know better – went from carriage to carriage with a set of bongo drums, a battered guitar, a kazoo and a repertoire of just two songs. One was 'This Train is Going to Richmond, This Train', which they'd reverse when necessary to, 'This Train is Going to Barking, This Train'. The other number was their signature protest song about shaving in toilets. It referred to the time when they were homeless and used to wash in public conveniences. The practice was banned and led them to pen lyrics, which included: 'If you can't have a shave in the toilet, where can you have a shave?/Think of all the other things that people do in toilets/Much worse than shaving/Dirtier than raving/We only want to keep ourselves clean and respectable/clean and respecta-bul!' Then they'd go around the tube carriage with a small omelette pan to collect money, saying that they accepted 'cash, cheques, luncheon vouchers and Indian rupees'.

Since busking became official, they've been forced onto the mainline network, which they didn't like as much. Watching them wander through the crowded aisles of a South West Trains' carriage after singing their new song, 'This Train is Going to Reading, This Train', it was obvious that their hearts were not in it. Indeed, the shorter of the two once slammed some small change back into the lap of a 'fan', obviously finding it offensive to receive coppers, muttering, 'Anything dangerous and controversial is banned. They just support wallflowers at the bottom of escalators and call that art. That's not art.' He then stormed off in an artistic strop.

How to be a busker

You might fancy strutting your stuff on London's biggest stage in the hope that you'll be spotted by some pop Svengali, but remember that this has not happened to any London Underground buskers in recent years – unless you count the Opera Babes (and they were at Covent Garden piazza, not in the Tube itself). If you remain determined, follow these tips for success.

'When will I, will I, be famous?'

• Get a good pitch. We're not talking about the pitch of your voice here (although that helps). It really is worth going for a London Underground audition and being official, as you get the best pitches or spots at stations. Over 55 million commuters pass the spots at Oxford Circus each year.

• Don't think winning the Mercury Music Prize is going to help you. Woolly-hatted warbler Badly Drawn Boy (Damon Gough to his mum) has sold millions of albums and, in 2000, won the prestigious Mercury Music Prize. When he decided to do a bit of busking in the video for 'All Possibilities', three years later, he set up outside Waterloo station, where secret cameras filmed him. Over 90 minutes he played his heart out to a stream of indifferent commuters and made a paltry £4.90.

• Move to Switzerland. The website Eurobuskers www.eurobuskers.free.fr conducted a survey to find out which European country is the most generous in paying street musicians. Taking critical factors into account, like the cost of living in the country concerned, seasonal changes and the percentage of tourists, it appears that Switzerland is the best place to busk, followed by Ireland. The UK manages third place – so there's hope for you budding London buskers.

• Get yourself an instant band. It's possible to buy recordings of popular songs with the lead instrument or vocals removed. You play along with your guitar, saxophone, harp, kazoo, comb-and-paper, traffic cone or whatever instrument has taken your fancy. Alternatively, you can go hi-tech and buy a piece of software to do this for you. Some programs will even slow down the music if you're a bit rusty and don't want to play several bars behind the original track.

Please move inside the carriages so everyone can board the train. I know it is a bit squashy, but you never know, you might make a new friend to spend the weekend with.

New songs for buskers

Instead of turning out endless, painful versions of 'Wonderwall' and 'Streets of London', perhaps buskers would do better if they played some songs inspired by Tube station names. Here's the top ten stationary tunes for buskers on the move:

'Waterloo' (Abba)

'Baker Street' (Gerry Rafferty)

'Angel(s)' (Robbie Williams)

'Plaistow Patricia' (Ian Dury and the Blockheads)

'Dagenham [East or Heathway] Dave' (Morrissey)

'Let Barking Dogs Lie' (Hawkwind)

'Highgate Shuffle' (Rod Stewart)

'Rumpus in Richmond' (Duke Ellington)

'The Only Living Boy in New Cross' (Carter the Unstoppable Sex Machine)

'Limehouse Blues' (Douglas Furber and Philip Braham)

Further reading

There are simply hundreds of music books with unique arrangements for buskers, including *Buskers 21st Century Pop*, *Buskers 21st Century Rock* (both published by Music Sales Limited) and *Busking for Special Occasions* (Wise Publications). Check out a computer program called *Transkriber* (made by Reed Kotler software) if you want to slow down music to learn the licks.

Street musicians have fascinated literary observers of London life for years and their work provides a great way to discover what busking was like before it was legalised:

'For what they are worth, I want to give my opinions about the life of a London busker. When one comes to think of it, it is strange that some people in a great modern city should spend their waking hours playing recorders in hot dens underground. The question I am raising is why this life goes on – what purpose it serves, and who wants it to continue, and why?' George Orwell, *Down and Out in London and Paris* (Penguin).

'First he played the little air from *The Magic Flute* by which Tamino fetches the beasts out of the forest. The thought came to him that he too was trying to summon beasts from a jungle, these people in this subterranean place, many of whose faces looked to him bestial, mad or very wretched.' Barbara Vine, *King Solomon's Carpet* (Penguin).

'We returned to the station to find in one of the underground corridors with superb acoustics, Rachel, an attractive lass from St John's Wood, was already deep into the first movement of Beethoven's "Violin Concerto in D Major" with its superb octaval leaps and G string twiddly bits.' John Hillaby, *John Hillaby's London* (Constable).

I apologise for the delay, caused by trying to fit too many trains onto too little track.

A busker trying to charm money into his bag.

6 Next stop Hollywood – celebrities on the Tube

From A list to Z list to Amma from *Big Brother 2*, London's stuffed with celebs who have to get to their recording studios, theatres and parties. The Tube's an obvious choice of travel. It's central, it's fast, it's – well, it's central. But just how likely are you to be (strap) hanging with the Queen, Kevin Spacey and other famous Londoners? Will you be making eyes at Hugh Grant or have your face squashed in the armpit of that bloke from the Iceland advert?

According to the *Evening Standard*, 'London is the only city in Britain where the rich and successful use public transport in numbers. Driving your big, fat car into the middle of town is most definitely not "funky" and incipient gridlock is making that increasingly obvious.' The columnist claims to have spotted the derrières of Jonathan Miller, Edward Fox, Sir Anthony Hopkins, Julian Barnes and Tony Banks all gracing Tube seats. Yeah, right. Along with Lord Lucan, the Roswell alien and Shergar.

The truth is that the rich and famous would rather stick Cuban cigars in their eyes than use the Tube. But if they have to go Underground, these days there's usually a celebrity spin doctor standing in the ticket queue, trying to get change from a pony.

Right: *Prince Charles always wanted to be a train driver.*

The Prime Minister

It seemed like a good idea back in October 1999. That notable Man of the People, Tony Blair, decided he would simply use the Tube. The message was straightforward. 'I'm a Londoner. I travel on the Tube each day because I want to avoid all the congestion.'

Nobody tipped off London Underground who remained 'completely unaware', they said, of his impromptu trip on the Jubilee Line. Along with chief spin doctor Alastair Campbell, Blair took several bodyguards, a rabid pack of journalists and a bundle of photographers onto the Tube. Even this impressive mob failed to impact on the Zen-like ability of Tube staff to ignore the world around them.

After scoring his own ticket, Mr Blair boarded a fairly empty carriage and sat next to a woman at random. He flashed her his trademark Colgate grin. Nothing. He said, 'Hi!' in a friendly fashion. Still nothing. For, like any reasonable commuter, the woman had decided to blank this animated fellow, knowing that only utter psychos smile at you on the Tube.

Although plenty of seats were available, pictures of Tony standing up were bagged by the gleeful press as he performed what looked like a seductive pole dance in the middle of the carriage while casually reading, as you do, a Government White Paper on transport. All of this frantic activity failed to elicit even a glimmer of recognition from the lone woman passenger, who seemed hypnotised by the toons on her walkman.

Undeterred, Mr Blair gestured in the direction of the accompanying photographers and said: 'I am sorry about all this.' By the time the woman got off at Canary Wharf, a deflated no-mates Blair had resorted to shuffling through his papers and asking Alastair Campbell's opinion about Burnley's chances in the FA Cup. The People's Prime Minister should know that people ignore each other on the Tube. It's the law. And it doesn't matter who you are, you're never gonna change it.

> **Sorry for the delay, but there has been an incident at King's Cross. Someone has attacked the driver. It's 9.15 am on a Monday morning and there's been an incident already. The police have been called. It's a good thing I'm not a policeman, because I'd lock them all up for life. Either that or shoot them.**

The Queen

Her Maj was first pictured on the Underground when she was only 12 years old. The experience wasn't to be repeated until 30 years had passed and she opened great-great-granny's Line – otherwise known as the Victoria Line.

Being the daughter of the world's most famous Cockney (the late Queen Elizabeth the Queen Mum – Gawd bless 'er) the Tube was an obvious mode of transport for the plucky princess. Like all 12-year-olds, young Liz was highly excited by the prospect of travelling on an escalator. She was pictured bounding down the steps at Tottenham Court Road, calculating how many bars of Fruit-and-Nut she'd be able to get out of the Cadbury's chocolate machine with her pocket money.

Princess Margaret was also seen in the picture, skipping downstairs while calculating how many packets of Players No 6 she'd be able to get out of the cigarette machine. This was at a time when smoking was still allowed on the

Tube. Now the only pollution comes from badly-busked versions of 'American Pie' and 'Waterloo Sunset'. Following the Royal adventure in the Tube, the Queen Mum was also pictured – with 50 packets of wine gums in her bag, confiscated from Margaret the little minx. Having discovered that the fag machine was broken, Mags had decided to see exactly just how much wine was in each gum.

> **May I remind all passengers that there is strictly no smoking allowed on any part of the Underground. However, if you are smoking a joint, it is only fair that you pass it round the rest of the carriage.**

One even travelled third class.

How to spot a wannabe

So, you've resigned yourself to the fact that you're just not likely to see many celebrities on the Tube, but follow this handy guide and you'll be able to spot those who may in the future be gracing our glossy mags, silver screens and album covers.

Well, well, well, ladies and gentlemen, it's happened again. Delays on your Victoria Line and all sorts of trouble on the Jubilee. God only knows what's going on there. It's gonna take more than Ken Livingstone to sort the Tube out.

The theatre student

How to recognise them: they will not be on their own. These girls (and they're always girls) travel in noisy packs. They normally have long blonde hair and wear pink, yellow and sky blue or any dayglo colour to 'blend in'.

Most likely to be reading: a script at 200 decibels. Delivered with a woodenness that Pinocchio would be proud of. The cut-glass tone they're trying for is that of Gwyneth Paltrow, but unfortunately they sound more like Hyacinth Bucket.

Most likely to board at: St John's Wood, Hampstead and Kilburn – the homes of spoilt, middle-class princesses.

Most likely to get off at: Clapham North for the Italia Conti Academy of Theatre Arts, Marylebone for the Sylvia Young Theatre School or the Angel for the Anna Scher Children's Theatre.

The jobbing actor

How to recognise them: will be wearing a tweed jacket with a cravat, a paisley scarf or a striped, woollen scarf and a hat. It does not matter if they are male or female, the look is always the same. Picture them with a packet of Daz, Wotsits or indigestion tablets in their hands and you'll know exactly why they look so familiar from TV.

Most likely to be reading: *The Stage* – what else, darling?

Most likely to board at: Chalk Farm. Well, it's so close to the wonderful Roundhouse. Darling.

Most likely to get off at: Piccadilly Circus for Shaftesbury Avenue and Theatreland. You can almost smell the greasepaint when you arrive (darling). Alternatively, the same station, but for the rather less exalted ad agencies of Golden Square who handle all those car insurance voiceovers.

The record producer/superstar DJ/rap artist

How to recognise them: You will know them by their Apple iBooks, loaded with the latest music software and graphics to show each pulse of their newest tune. They're probably also plugged into an enormous set of headphones normally only seen on air traffic controllers.

Most likely to be reading: *Mixmag* or *Jockey Slut*.

Most likely to board at: Brixton, Walthamstow East or any other station mentioned in lyrics by the Streets.

Most likely to get off at: Brixton, Walthamstow East or another Tube station where their friend from the Streets is also working.

The politician

How to recognise them: Crisp white shirt, Saville Row pin-striped suit and a pair of trainers to show how 'street' they are.

Most likely to be reading: The latest kiss-and-tell political autobiography or 'novel' by Edwina Curry (to see if they can spot themselves).

Most likely to board at: Richmond, Kew Gardens, Wimbledon or Sloane Square, despite being the MP for Haringey, Lewisham or another inner London Borough.

Most likely to get off at: Westminster, for the home of democracy, a hotbed of political ideas, or Piccadilly Circus, for Soho, the home of many hot beds.

> This is information for passengers waiting on platform two. There is no information. I'm hoping to have some soon and as soon as I do, I'll let you have it.

The footballer

How to recognise them: Top of the range Adidas or Nike tracksuit. Thin hair from too many hair colourants, with a cut that's David Beckham's last-but-one style.

Most likely to be reading: the *Sun*, the *Mirror* or the *Star*. Not the sports sections, but the 'news' section with its pages of scantily clad ladies, where they hope to spot a previous or future conquest.

Most likely to board: more little league than premiere league if still travelling by Tube, so Dagenham East for Dagenham and Redbridge FC, or Bounds Green for the Crouch End Vampires.

Most likely to get off at: Fulham Broadway for Chelsea's Stamford Bridge, Highbury for Arsenal's Highbury or Seven Sisters for Spurs' White Hart Lane. 'Live your dreams', as the sportswear companies say.

To many people, the Tube actually represents London itself. Remember the old films in which double-decker buses were used to show that the story had moved to London? Now those old double-deckers have been replaced by the Underground. Countless hip and trendy films show people coming in and out of Tube stations and focus on the world famous logo. The Tube has even had a starring role in some films.

There have been horror flicks set in the Tube, among them *An American Werewolf in London*, a gory take on the annoying Yank tourist theme. Mornington Crescent even inspired a game on the long-running radio show *I'm Sorry I Haven't a Clue* and the Underground has been an inspiration to many TV shows. Let's just hope the Tube doesn't get above itself and demand a dressing room.

> **Due to an overpowering smell of sewage, this train will not be stopping at Highgate. I repeat, this train will not stop at Highgate... Ladies and gentlemen, this train is stopping at Highgate and, of course, I'm the last to know.**

Right: *Likely Lad, James Bolam, plays an unlikely driver in* First Sign of Madness.

Making an entrance

In *Sliding Doors*, Gwyneth Paltrow aired an uncanny London accent and endeared herself to the Brits with a dilemma we all face. What would have happened to your life if you had caught the Tube that you just missed by a few seconds? Would it have changed? Would you have met the person of your dreams or just sat next to a nutter? Those vital seconds have a crucial role for her character and the film shows her alternative lives with dramatically different outcomes. *Sliding Doors* was a big hit on both sides of the Atlantic but other broadcasts starring the Tube haven't fared so brilliantly.

This is like that TV advert, I hope the person next to you is wearing a good deodorant.

Don't mind the gap

You'll be hard pushed to remember a TV quiz show called *Mind the Gap*. Doesn't really sound like a winning format. Take one 'personality': Paul Ross (older brother of the far more famous Jonathan). Throw in a set that mirrors a Tube tunnel, an annoying voiceover repeating 'M-m-m-mind the gap' ad nauseum and top it all with three contestants pitting their wits against each other with the time-honoured fingers on the buzzer format. It was commissioned for just one series and even then was only limited to London's Carlton TV. Perhaps it might one day make it to Challenge TV, with any luck, and be broadcast with *Supermarket Sweep*, *Pets Win Prizes* and *Touch the Truck* at 3 am. Perfect for insomniacs.

Minardors

Tube troglodytes – half-human creatures – starred in the early-1970s horror flick *Death Line* or *Raw Meat* (its title across the pond). The trogs lived under Russell Square station and feasted on people. Donald Pleasance

Above: *Paul Ross straddling the famous gap.*

played Inspector Culhorn, a crusty old British detective from Scotland Yard investigating the latest disappearance. There was a two-minute cameo role from Hammer Horror stalwart Christopher Lee, but the main star was the violent, long-haired, living-dead Tube trog. The premise was that a group of Victorian workers had been trapped underground when a tunnel collapsed and were never rescued due to budgetary constraints (Ken Livingstone take note). The only phrase aside from grunts that these poor unfortunates mastered was 'Mind the doors'.

> **The good news is that last Friday was my birthday and I hit the town and had a great time. I felt let down by the fact that none of you sent me a card. I drive you to work and home each day and not even a card.**

Perhaps the film was influenced by an episode of *The Goon Show* in the 1950s called 'The Scarlet Capsule'. The radio show was a parody of another classic British sci-fi series, *Quartermass and the Pit*, in which excavations uncover skeletons of a previously unknown species of human. Now that sounds familiar:

Willium: Then I hears an hissing sound, and a voice says, 'Minardor'.
Quatermass: 'Minardor'? We must keep our ears, nose and throats open for anything that goes 'minardor'.
Bannister: Yes.
Crun: Be forewarned, sir, the minardor is an ancient word that can be read in the West of Minster's library, you know.
Quatermass: Well, it so happens that I have a Westminster Library on me. And gad, look! There I am inside, examining an occult dictionary.
Bannister: Oh, yes.
Quatermass: Minardor… minardor… hmm, hmm, hmm… Min, min, min, min, min…
Bannister: Yes, yes, yes, yes, yes?
Quatermass: I feel an attack of conks coming on. Quick, the brandy!

"Genuine thrills! In the best of horror film traditions!"
— Gene Vickel, Chicago Tribune

Above: *Anything to escape the rush hour.*

Thanks to author Neil Gaiman for bringing the play to our attention. As well as being the writer of cult graphic novel *Sandman* and too many other successful books, screenplays and biographies to mention, Neil has penned his own London Underground classic in the shape of *Neverwhere*.

Neverwhere

Originally a BBC2 fantasy series co-produced with comedian Lenny Henry, *Neverwhere* later became a best-selling novel. The Tube is a key character in the story. A strange London Below is uncovered in *Neverwhere*, where real nobility resides where there are just stations in our world, Barons Court and Earl's Court. There are knights at Knightsbridge and a monastery at Blackfriars. The Earl and overlord of the transport system in London Below holds his court in one of those darkened special trains that periodically zoom through the capital. 'Stand back, train approaching – this train will not be stopping here' comes over the PA system and passengers stand back, sighing, as the darkened carriages hurtle through the station. Perhaps if you look a little closer into the black windows in future, you may see some of those strange underground creatures which populate films, radio and TV.

> **We have what is technically known as a Frank Spencer Situation... Hmm Betty, we've got a little bit of trouble.**

Travelling on the Tube is a game of chance in the face of unknown obstacles: station closures, overcrowding, delays, getting stuck in tunnels, delays, platform changes, escalators, lifts breaking down and more delays. You may as well be travelling in a giant board game, with twists, turns and tasks at every corner. Funnily enough, *The London Game* is a real board game in which the fun comes from mirroring the joys of Tube travel and dodging the daily hazards.

For those who don't find the real thing to be such an enjoyable game, there are some insider tricks for you to learn to ensure your survival on the Tube. You'll soon be able to face any hazard and complete your journey in the most pleasant way possible. You might not win *The London Game* but you will develop your skills in navigation, time management, perseverance, inner calm, instant character judgement and clairvoyance.

I apologise for the delay but the computer controlling the signalling has the Monday morning blues.

In through the out door

You're running late. You've only got a minute spare to catch your connecting train or a minute to make that vital appointment. How do you make up the lost time? If only you could be sure of being near the exit or way out signs when you leave. If only someone could tell you where to get on to get off. Despair no more. The handy *Way Out Tube Map* by Roger Collings (Drumhouse Ltd) does exactly that. It's an ingenious crib sheet that shows which carriage arrives directly by the exit at your chosen destination. Once you've spent an hour working out how to use it, you'll never be at the wrong end of the station again.

How to get in front of the opening doors

You've been waiting ages for a train. The platform is becoming more and more crowded. Finally, the train pulls in. You see empty carriages sail past, but all those near you are looking full. The train's about to come to a halt, but where exactly will it stop? It's that classic *Wheel of Fortune* moment. The doors hover tantalisingly before you. Will they

stop in front of you? They get closer and closer. Fifty other people around you eye the way into the carriage with exactly the same thoughts in mind. Then the train takes that extra lurch and moves on a foot and you've missed the doors. You are forced to squeeze on at the end, frustrated, annoyed and bemoaning the unfairness of it all.

Bemoan no more. In order to achieve MSDA (Maximum Sliding Door Alignment), simply stand In front of the 'Mind the gap' signs painted on the floor. The doors will most often open neatly in front of you. If there are no signs, stand where the paint from the yellow or white platform edge lines looks more faded and scuffed – a sure-fire indicator of passenger departure wear and tear.

Ladies and gentlemen, this train has 22 doors on each side. Please feel free to use all of them, not just the two in the middle.

Please move along the platform.

Strap-hanging builds up your biceps.

How to avoid strap-hanging

If you've followed MSDA on page 83, you will be in a good position to get a seat, as getting on first gives you a chance to race for any empty places or to get ready to grab one when it becomes available.

Another trick involves standing in the middle of the rows of seats rather than hanging around with the cool, trendy and nonchalant commuters by the door. If you stay in the door ghetto, you'll have no chance of getting a seat as the carriage gets more crowded.

Stand near people who look as though they are about to get off soon. This may sound as though you need the powers of Mystic Meg, but is much simpler than having eyes that go in different directions or never leaving the house without a crystal ball and pack of tarot cards. All you need to do is think about what people are likely to be doing – those, for example, with big rucksacks and luggage are likely to get off at major train stations such as King's Cross,

Next stop Euston?

There is a security alert and we are stuck here for the foreseeable future. Let's take our minds off it and pass some time together. All together now... Ten, green bottles standing on a wall ...

Victoria and Euston. If you're really good at this, you can listen out for accents – a Northern twang means they'll be heading back home via Euston.

Watch out for Pre-Departure Shuffling (PDS). Passengers fortunate enough to have that seat you've got your eye on will start to fidget shortly before they have to get off. They'll be putting away their books or newspapers, wrapping up Walkman leads and checking they still have their umbrella. Remember for your own PDS routine that this is to be done not more than one stop before departure – you shouldn't give the wrong signals to fellow seat hunters.

Once you've correctly identified passengers who are about to depart, you'll need to manoeuvre yourself into a good position to slide effortlessly into the seat the moment it's vacated. Bear in mind that a growing number of commuters learn these techniques, but Tube etiquette states that whoever is nearest to the seat has the greatest claim. It's first come, first served on the Tube.

How to spot seats not worth having

Every person travelling for more than one stop will take a seat that is empty (unless they are a Labour politician or the Mayor doing a photo shoot). So if you get onto a full carriage and find an empty seat, there is likely to be a very good reason for its emptiness.

What's on your seat? People leave all manner of unpleasant deposits behind them. A recent urban legend had thousands of commuters believing that a team of forensic scientists found the following in the fibres of a tube seat: four types of hair (human, mouse, rat and dog), seven types of insect (mostly fleas), vomit (from nine separate people), four samples of urine, human and rodent excrement and worse. It turned out to be a spoof report, but you will find chewing gum, leftover kebabs, alcohol, vomit, leftover burgers and unidentifiable brown stains on any number of seats.

Who's sitting next to you? You may just have got on, but people who've been travelling for several

'I wonder why that seat's empty?'

stops have by now spotted the drunk, that person with a very loud Walkman or the nutter who will insist on talking to you the moment you slide into the space next to them. It's easy to spot the people who kindly share their toons with the rest of the carriage – you'll hear them and see their large headphones. Anyone clutching a can of Tennants Extra or Diamond White between 9am and 10.30am can quickly be identified as a drunk or a City broker.

Nutters – that's anyone who strikes up a noisy, embarrassing conversation with whoever sits next to them – are the most difficult to identify. You can spot the following tell-tale signs. They mumble to themselves, rehearsing the surreal conversation they will have with you. They're likely not to be reading anything. They may be singing with no sign of a Walkman's headphones. They'll be distracted and fidgeting for several stops (not to be confused with the PDS described on page 86). They'll be wearing a T-shirt several times too small for them. They are likely to be male – beware, female passengers who strike up conversations with strangers are even more worrying.

Avoid the scream – staying sane when stuck in a tunnel

Stopping between stops is as inevitable on the Tube as toast falling butter side down. The majority of unscheduled stops will be in a tunnel, with nothing to see outside the window but blackness. If you haven't got a book or a paper, there is nothing to do but stare at the ads or at your fellow commuters.

TS Eliot recorded this existential problem perfectly in his poem 'East Coker': 'Or as, when an Underground train, in the Tube, stops too long between stations/And the conversation rises and slowly fades into silence/And you see

> **Apologies for the delay but we have lost power to the train, as you can tell by the blinding speed at which we're travelling.**

Do __not__ worry about power failure.

behind every face the mental emptiness deepen/Leaving only the growing terror of nothing to think about.' That's not quite true. Most people will actually be thinking: 'How long are we going to be stuck and how late will I be now?' When the sticking lasts longer than the usual two or three minutes, you will need to avoid growing terror by using some tested sanity preservation techniques:

• Imagine that you are alone in a large quiet room and not in a small metal carriage surrounded by hundreds of other people. Do not imagine that this is the last train you will ever catch, that you are about to suffocate with strangers or that everyone else is staring at you for some unknown reason. These natural thoughts are very counter-productive to your sanity.

- Look at an area above everyone else's head. In this way you won't notice the man or woman opposite you, trying to avoid your vacant stare. You'll also avoid the panic-struck look of novice Tube travellers who will be starting to shuffle and fidget.

- If the seat opposite you is empty, you have a good opportunity to test the strength of your eye muscles and try to evoke pictures from the patterns in the seat. Magic Eye, the people who created the mid-1990s 3-d picture craze, obviously spent a lot of time on the Tube. Try not to do this for too long, as your eyes will start to cross.

- Count backwards from a thousand. If you get to single digits, panic – you've been in the tunnel too long.

Step right this way for the sauna, ladies and gentlemen... Towels are not provided.

It's getting hot in here

You may have thought that after the best part of two hundred years of the Tube being around, climate control would be under control. It's not. Mayor Ken Livingstone even issued a £100,000 reward for the person who could invent a successful way to cool the tube. So until the day pigs start flying, you will have to cope with stifling temperatures in the summer months – Dockland station names East India and West India Quay are not totally inappropriate.

We fare no better in the winter, as a team of cold-blooded station controllers pump up the underground's heaters to toasty levels, giving us all pneumonia when we step into the freezing winds above ground. Be prepared for these changes in temperature with this check list:

- Layers of clothing. It's always easy to add and take off clothing, so start with the bare minimum that you would be prepared to go out in. Add layers of lightweight, breathable clothing to a bag so you're equally prepared

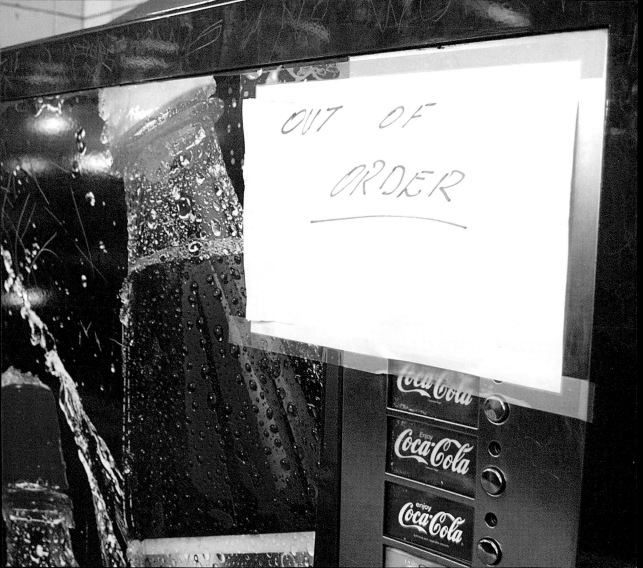

for a day out in St Tropez or an icy trek in St John's Wood.

• Bottle of water. For those occasions when you might get stuck in a tunnel and need to stop your body's loss of water. In the summer, you'll be sweating heavily and in winter a cold sweat (caused by worrying whether rescue teams will get through the ice) will have a similar effect.

• Copy of *Metro* or other tabloid newspaper. Use this as a fan in the summer and tear pages out of it in the winter to use as insulation for your shoes. Broadsheet newspapers should be banned on the Tube, as there is precious little space in the rush hour to avoid taking someone's eye out in your effort to turn the pages of a big paper.

• Sandals and trainers. No commuter is complete without his or her Tube-issue pair of Birkenstock sandals for hot days. Sporty trainers are also essential, as you'll always be running due to delays caused by Tube tracks buckling in the summer heat or freezing in the winter.

The end of the line

Before we all change, let's be like futurologist Professor Archibald Montgomery Low, who we met in the Tube's chronology, and make predications for the way the Tube will look in 75 years.

There will be four new tube lines: the Southern Line, the William Line (after King William), the M25 Line (can't be slower than travelling on the motorway equivalent) and the Cockerdoodleloo Line (joining Cockfosters to Waterloo). All trains will have air conditioning and carriages will secrete pleasant wafts of lavender oil to ease commuters gently into the morning (or relax on the way home). Finally, free copies of this book will be given away as a piece of history, showing the mad and crazy ways of those funny people at the turn of the century.

The Bakerloo Line is running normally today, so you may expect delays to all destinations.

Just why do we do it?

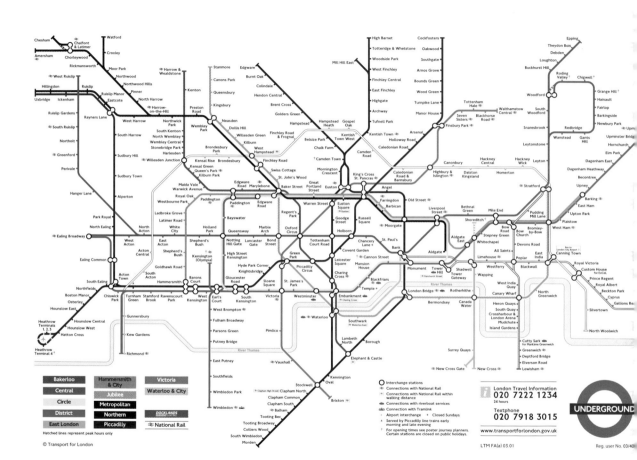

Author acknowledgements

For her tireless and sometimes tiresome research, my friend Annie Mole, webmistress of www.goingunderground.net

For his support throughout the early stages of this book, my ex husband, Peter Kenny, www.peterkenny.co.uk

For providing excellent cartoons, Ralf Zeigermann, The Insekt Ltd, www.ralfz.dsl.pipex.com

For illustrating the tube driver comedian, Russell Becker, www.russellbecker.com

For some photographic inspiration, Simon James, www.simonjames.co.uk

Finally, for everyone who has travelled with me daily from Kew Gardens to Piccadilly Circus, thank you for making the journey almost bearable.

Picture credits

Atlantic Syndication: p65
Reproduced courtesy of Carlton International Media: p78
Carlton Television: p75, p77
Ken Garland: p42
Hulton Archive: p39, p40
Mecca Ibrahim: p34, P44, p82 (bottom), p87
Simon James: p47
London Transport Museum: p8, p12, p13, p25, p27, P46, p52, p63, p67, p80, p83, p8
Annie Mole: p48, p49, p85
Eddie Mulholland: p17
Duncan Soar: Front and back cover, p1, p2, p3, p7, p11, p15, p19, p20, p23, p28, p29, p30, p35, P45, p53, p54, p55, p56, p57, p61, p59, p81, p82 (top), p84, p88, p91, p93, p94

Artwork credits

Russell Becker: p9
Ralf Zeigermann: p22, p24, p26, p32-33, p50, p51, p69, p70, p71, p72, p73

First published in 2004 by
New Holland Publishers (UK) Ltd
London • Cape Town • Sydney • Auckland
www.newhollandpublishers.com

Garfield House
86-88 Edgware Road
London W2 2EA
United Kingdom

80 McKenzie Street
Cape Town 8001
South Africa

Level 1, Unit 4
Suite 411, 14 Aquatic Drive
Frenchs Forest, NSW 2086
Australia

218 Lake Road
Northcote
Auckland
New Zealand

10 9 8 7 6 5 4 3 2 1

Publishing Manager: Jo Hemmings
Project Editor: Camilla MacWhannell
Designer: Ian Hughes
Production: Joan Woodroffe

Reproduction by Modern Age Repro House Ltd,
  Hong Kong
Printed in Singapore by Star Standard Industries
  Pte Ltd

ISBN 1 84330 708 1